Perspectives & Praise
for
7 Weeks to a Better American Accent for Native Mandarin Speakers—Volume 1

"Many native Chinese speakers can master English grammar but are not able to get rid of their accent no matter how many years they practice. Tracey's book offers a well laid out 7 week course that could improve your communication with native English speakers dramatically."

Sam Fong

"Pretty good guide and well organized."

Li Lei

"I read the book sample. It's great. I had the same problems of arriving to the United States and could not understand what others were talking about when I got off the plane. The pronunciation is totally different than what I learned in China. In addition if courses were offered to match the book, it would be even better."

Xiaoying (Angela) Yang

"Speaking English is always frustrating for us Mandarin native speakers. However it will be a totally different story if we really master those tricks with an insider's help. I am glad that Tracey wrote this book just for us. She knows well of the difference between Mandarin and English and gives very good advice on how to improve English accent in a short period. I would like to recommend this book to my Chinese fellows, hoping they will enjoy speaking English and benefit from their new American English accent."

Lin Gong, M.E. Former Language Teacher

"Even if you're on the right track, you'll get run over if you just sit there."

Will Rogers

7 Weeks to a Better American Accent for Native Mandarin Speakers
Volume 1

Tracey Ingram, M.A., M.S.

Sovereign Language Press
www.sovereignlanguagepress.com

7 weeks to a Better American Accent for Native Mandarin Speakers, Volume 1© 2010

All rights Reserved.
Published & Printed in the United States by Sovereign Language Press, Chicago.
www.sovereignlanguagepress.com

Grateful acknowledgment is made to The Handbook of the International Phonetics Association corporate author: International Phonetic Association Cambridge University Press, New York ©, 1999. Reprinted with permission.

No part of this publication may be reproduced, stored in a retrieval system, or transmitted, in any form or by any means (mechanical, electronic, photocopying, recording, or otherwise), without prior written permission of both the copyright owner and the publisher of this book.

The scanning, uploading, and distribution of this book via Internet or via any other means without the permission of the publisher is illegal and punishable by law. Please purchase only authorized electronic editions and do not participate in or encourage electronic piracy of copyrightable materials. Your support of the author's rights is greatly appreciated.

All inquiries should be addressed to:
Sovereign Language Press, Inc.
28 E. Jackson Blvd #10-A850
Chicago, IL. 60604
http://www.sovereignlanguagepress.com

ISBN- 978-0-615-40686-2

Library of Congress Control Number: 2010914676

Book design by Sue Balcer, justyourtype.biz

A portion of author's royalties will be donated to nonprofit organizations dedicated to inspiring, educating, and empowering women and young girls.

About the Author

Ms. Tracey Ingram, M.A., M.S., is the Founder & Global Communication Specialist of the Institute of Accent Modification, located in Chicago, Illinois, where she works with students and professionals in American accent training and communication skills development workshops. She is certified by the Institute of Language and Phonology to provide accent modification training to foreign born professionals. She and her team utilize an integrative and customized approach to helping their clients achieve their goals and objectives.

In August 2010, the Institute of Accent Modification, received a business development grant from the National Association for the Self Employed (NASE), to expand the business. Tracey Ingram is nationally certified by the American Speech Language Hearing Association (ASHA), and is also a member of ITBE (Illinois Teachers of English to Speakers of Other Languages).

Before becoming a Global Communication specialist, Ms. Ingram maintained a private clinical Audiology practice specializing in providing mobile audiology services to seniors in the Chicagoland area. She has also consulted with several area small businesses and Fortune 500 companies regarding their employee's communication needs. She has also been a consultant with several area colleges and universities, including Dominican University, Elmhurst College, and DePaul University. She has been a frequently invited guest speaker to local and national healthcare organizations.

- Workshops for all individuals on communication & presentation skills
- Customized individual & group workshops on American accent training
- Programs available worldwide in our online meeting centers
- Available for consultation
- Visit the website for programs www.instituteofaccentmodification.com
- Visit my blog page for current articles, tips, and newsletter signup http://blog.instituteofaccentmodification.com
- Follow me on Twitter @Globalaccentpro
- Become a Fan of the Institute of Accent Modification on Facebook http://bit.ly/auCzxZ

Dedication

*This book is dedicated to my loving parents,
Carl Edward and Helen Marie Ingram,
who've always listened and encouraged me
to dream big and work hard.
I love you both.*

Table of Contents

		MP3 Audio	page
	Introduction	Track 1	15
Week 1	Production of Speech	Track 2	21
	American Consonant sounds	Track 3	22
	American Vowel sounds	Track 4	23
	Consonants and vowels	Track 5	24
	How vowels are produced	Track 6	29
Week 2	Sharpening your Listening Skills	Track 7	33
	Vowel speech discrimination	Track 8	35
	Consonant speech discrimination	Track 9	39
Week 3	Word Associations & contractions	Track 10	45
Week 4	Importance of Intonation	Track 11	47
Week 5	Practice Stories	Track 12	54
	"R" Practice Story	Track 13	55
	"L" Practice Story	Track 14	56
Week 6	Idiomatic Expressions	Track 15	57
Week 7	Advanced Vocabulary	Track 16	60
	Resources		63
	Bonus Material		64

Acknowledgements

I would like to acknowledge Arthur J. Compton, Ph,D. of the Institute of Language and Phonology for the development of the Compton P-ESL program. I'd like to personally thank Elinor Stutz for her inspiration and positive attitude. I'd like to thank my assistant, Meng Ge, the editor, publisher, typesetter, book cover design team, and my sister for working countless hours on this project. I'd like to thank my close friends who were there to listen and cheer me on!

I would like to acknowledge my loyal Mandarin speaking clients and the Mandarin forum group, who read the stories, followed the exercises in this guide, and provided valuable feedback. Their honest feedback helped to make this publication possible and will allow this training format to be available worldwide. Thank you all so much.

Tracey Ingram

INTRODUCTION   TRACK 1

The ability to communicate effectively is vital in today's globalized world. I have always been personally very fascinated by communication. As I continued with my graduate studies and started to travel internationally, I realized that cross culturally, we all have a need to be understood.

I have worked professionally as a clinical Audiologist for many years and wanted to expand my services by offering communication workshops for professionals. This idea later developed into the formation of the Institute of Accent Modification in Chicago, Illinois and working with foreign professionals to provide American accent training.

Let me clarify my opinion of accents. Everyone has an accent including some very famous people, which is a combination of intonation and pronunciation. The only time having an accent becomes a problem, is when you are not understood by others. As I began working with many native Mandarin speakers I developed this book, ***7 Weeks to a Better American Accent, for Native Mandarin Speakers - Volume 1*** to share with my clients and others, techniques to improve their accent.

WHY THIS BOOK IS DIFFERENT

You probably picked up this book wondering what makes this different than everything else on the market. First of all, this book is written by an American accent coach who has worked with many native Mandarin speakers. Over time, I have learned a lot about your fascinating culture and some of the most common challenges and error patterns you make when speaking American English. This program is intended primarily for individuals who have basic to intermediate skills regarding English grammar and vocabulary.

This is volume one of a fun new series of books whereby you will discover the secrets to making your conversational American English sound more fluid. The ultimate goal is to help you develop new speech habits and begin to use these habits in everyday situations as you continue with the series.

The way you previously learned English pronunciation is not the same way you learn to work on your accent. Conversational American English has a very smooth and fluid sound. It's not slow or awkward. Americans do not pronounce every single sound or word very carefully. In order to speak more fluidly and reduce your accent, you will need to modify some of the things you have been previously taught.

Changing some of your old habits takes time and initially, you will think a lot about how you speak. It's similar to learning how to dance for the first time. You are self conscious and feel awkward, but with practice, you become more comfortable and learn to relax. As you get more comfortable and start learning how to form word associations, you will sound much more natural and your confidence will start to increase.

There are several phases which will take place in this process. Initially, you will learn new sounds, correct English pronunciation, and get familiar with the rhythm and flow of speech. This initial phase of learning to hear new sounds and to discriminate which English sounds are difficult is critical. Learning how to hear these sounds correctly will help you tremendously with your English pronunciation.

It is important to practice several times a day for short periods of 10-15 minutes, focusing on listening and repetition to master this initial phase. After the initial phase, you will learn how to apply these principles in words, short phrases, and gradually sentences. Learning how to practice correctly with specialized training will take time and dedication. Finally, as you continue these new habits will start to automatically transfer in your everyday speech.

My Accent is bad, how can it be improved, and by the way, I was told that is it too late?

This is the most common question I hear when someone asks me what I do for a living. Everyone tells me they have been told that after a certain age it is impossible to change a person's accent. I am here to tell you that it can be done with diligent and focused practice, good materials, and a coach to provide customized guidance and feedback. I've had experience working with young college interns and older executives who have made measurable improvements in their accent or dialect.

When you are born and start learning your native language, you learn the language with ease and without thinking. When you learn another language, these rules you previously taught often act as an obstacle to the pronunciation of the new language. Mandarin is a precise language where word order is

Introduction

very strict. The words are never modified and everything is based on word order. Many of my Chinese students have mentioned that they did not previously have a lot of practice or feedback using spoken English prior to arriving to the United States.

> *When I first arrived from China, two years ago, to attend school in the United States, I felt that what I previously learned was very formulized and I discovered that's not how Americans speak. I initially joined a language exchange program at the school which helped a lot. Having a conversational language partner has helped my English pronunciation.*
> Meng Ge

When you start learning a second language, you often will experience much frustration and difficulty, trying to transfer what you previously were taught in a way that sounds like a Native American. You will notice, in the United States that the pronunciation varies from the West coast, South, or East Coast. You can have two people born from the same region who have a different accent. So, which accent is correct? The accent you presently have depends on your linguistic background. Even if you are fluent in English and have superb grammatical skills, your regional accent is strongly reflected in your speech.

WHAT THIS BOOK WILL DO FOR YOU

7 Weeks to a better American Accent for Native Mandarin Speakers (Volume 1) was written specifically for the Native Mandarin speaker to overcome language challenges while improving their spoken English. Each of the seven sections is divided by weeks. At the end of seven weeks, you will have completed the book. Every person is different and you should work at your own pace to achieve the level of competency that you desire.

Every language has its own sounds and pronunciation patterns. The information in this book helps to identify the "typically" challenging sounds of the Mandarin speaker. For example, there are several English sounds that do not occur in the Mandarin language. There are also many vowels and consonant sounds that have been difficult for Native Mandarin speakers to produce correctly.

I thought I was good when I left China for the United States to start my career. I had mastered all the lessons in my classes and was confident until the day I first arrived to the United States. When I got off the airplane, I had a hard time understanding the words that were spoken. The words sounded so fast. It was so overwhelming to me. To improve, I watched television in the evening and imitated the newscasters. I would also read local newspapers aloud every time I had a free moment. Liang Zhu, M.B.A.

This book will also discuss the importance of intonation and helpful word connections that will help the Mandarin speaker with fluency. If you find that you have completed most of this material and are still having difficulties, please refer to our resources in the back of the book which contain Bonus material. You can also call (888) 827-4479 to get your personalized comprehensive speech analysis and order additional materials.

It's important to have an American Accent coach to help you identify exactly which sounds and error patterns are contributing to your accent. An accent coach will analyze your speech and make suggestions that will save you a lot of time. A coach can teach you to hear the differences between words and customize a program to fit your needs. The accent you will learn in this program is that of standard American English. This is the way a professor lectures and news reporters announce the news throughout the day.

How to Use this Book and MP3 Recording

The book is recorded and the practice exercises can be repeated as often as necessary.

- You can start at the beginning of the book and gradually work your way through.
- The book has identified typical challenging sounds of the Mandarin language, and you can practice pronouncing each of the individual words containing the targeted sounds, using correct word stress and intonation patterns.

Introduction

- Highlight words and sounds that are difficult and practice pronunciation in front of a mirror or with a language partner.
- Practice words, sentences and paragraphs modeling the speaker on the audio until you are satisfied.
- Have a partner or trainer listen and critique you for additional help.

Format of the Sound Stories

- For additional practice there are stories which have the targeted sound with rules on pronunciation.
- You can prioritize the challenging sounds and listen to the recording, read each sentence aloud imitating what you have heard until you have mastered the desired sound.
- Read the stories and focus on a different goal each time, such as pronunciation, fluency, intonation, word endings, and linking word associations.
- Ask a native English speaker or accent coach to record you and to ask questions. Your goal is to sound as natural as possible.

Target Audience

- Non-native Chinese students
- Non-native Chinese professionals
- ESL and Chinese English Teachers

The Goals:

- Learn how to correctly pronounce American consonants and vowels
- Improve your listening skills and improve English accent
- Discover methods to improve voice projection
- Master intonation and the rhythm and flow of the American English language and the use of stress patterns
- Learn how to form word associations faster and improve your speaking rate
- Discover the secrets of using American idiomatic expressions in everyday conversations
- Tips on how to build an advanced level vocabulary

THE BENEFITS

- Improved job opportunities
- Reduce levels of frustration
- Improved interactions in business and personal life
- Increased work productivity
- Increased confidence speaking

Week 1

PRODUCTION OF SPEECH — TRACK 2

It is important to know how sounds are made before learning how to produce them. The sounds of the American English language are characterized by consonants and vowels. To discuss the sounds of the English language it is helpful to use phonetic symbols. These symbols used in this guide have been (adopted) from the International Phonetic Alphabet (IPA). This international system is utilized by linguists, researchers, and for teaching.

You will notice on the following pages the IPA symbols for consonant sounds and vowels along with an example word and phrase. There are only 6 vowel letters { a,e, i, o, u , and sometimes y} however there are 14 vowel sounds, which are called blends and clusters. Vowel sounds are voiced and usually are difficult to pronounce for most Mandarin speakers. You will want to listen to this section several times for your desired level of competency. Consonant sounds can be voiced and unvoiced.

The consonant and vowel symbols that are in **bold** type represent some of the most common error symbols with Mandarin speakers. Please keep in mind, there are always exceptions.

THE AMERICAN ENGLISH SOUND SYSTEM

Consonants Sounds

International Phonetic Symbols	English Equivalent	Word Example	Common word pairs
b	b	**b**oy	**B**ed and **b**reakfast
d	d	**d**og	**d**ay and night
f	f	**f**og	**f**ilthy rich
g	g	**g**old	**g**o crazy
h	h	**h**ello	**h**ave a drink
k	k	**k**ite	**k**eep the change
l	l	**l**ead	**l**ife or death
m	m	**m**ob	**m**ilk and cookies
n	n	tur**n**	It's my tur**n**
ŋ	ng	sa**ng**	play pi**ng**-po**ng**
p	p	**p**encil	**p**aper or **p**lastic?
r	r	**r**ose	**r**eady or not
s	s	**s**incere	**s**alt and pepper
ʃ	sh	**sh**eep	**sh**oes and socks
t	t	**t**ime	**t**all and **t**hin
θ	th (unvoiced)	**th**ink	put on your **th**inking cap
ð	th (voiced)	**th**is	**th**is and **th**at
v	v	**v**ery	**v**erbs and nouns
w	w	**w**ild	**w**ash and dry
y	y	**y**ell	**y**es and no
z	z	**z**oo	**z**igzag pattern
tʃ	ch	**ch**air	**ch**eese and macaroni
dʒ	dg	fu**dg**e	fu**dg**esicle pop

Week 1

THE AMERICAN ENGLISH SOUND SYSTEM — TRACK 4

Vowel Sounds

International Phonetic Symbols	English Equivalent	Word Example	Common word pairs
ɑ	o	pot	pots and pans
ʌ	u	luck	good luck
ae	a	tack	tick-tack-toe
e	a	make	make a sandwich
ɛ	e	debt	credit card debt
i	e	peach	peaches and cream
ɪ	I	hit	hit the books
ʊ	oo	foot	foot massage
u	oo	soon	sooner or later
o	o	sew	sewing machine
ə	u	upon	once upon a time
ɝ	er	bird	blackbird
ɚ	er	member	country club member
ɔ	aw	dawn	dawn of day

CONSONANTS & VOWELS — TRACK 5

HOW CONSONANTS ARE PRODUCED

It is important to understand that consonants are categorized by the following:

1. The place of production
2. The presence or absence of voicing
3. The manner of how sounds are produced

I. **Place of production**

The place and position of production focuses on the articulators which make the sound.

Dental - Sounds that involve the teeth are produced with the tongue resting between the teeth. The "th" sound is very challenging for Mandarin speakers. There is the unvoiced θ sound, such as "bath" and "thank", without the vocal cord vibration. The voiced ð sound, such as "then" and "mother", with the vocal cord vibration.

Labial - Sounds such {b, p, m, and w} can be produced at the lips (labial). The final "b" sound does not occur in the Mandarin language. The "p" and "b" are called stop consonants, and are made by stopping the air with the lips and having a quick release. The "m" sound is categorized as a nasal sound and it is produced as the airstream is directed through the nose. Practice the words, "move" and "merchandise". The "w" sound is formed by rounding the lips and directing the voiced airstream through your lips such as the words, "worried" and "waiting."

Alveolar - Sounds such as {l, z, s, n, d, t} can be produced by having the tip of the tongue sit behind the upper teeth. The final "t" and final "l" does not occur in the Mandarin language, so you will want to pay close attention to how these sounds are produced.

Palatal- Sounds such as {ʃ, dʒ, tʃ, j, and r} are produced with the tongue tip against the hard palate.

Velar – Sounds such as {g, ŋ, k} are produced with back of the tongue against the soft palate.

Glottal – The glottal sound such as "h" as in hurry is voiceless. The air is passed through the vocal folds. This sound does not occur in the Mandarin language.

II.   The Presence or Absence of voicing

Notice if the sound is voiced the vocal folds vibrate. If the sound is unvoiced the vocal folds do not vibrate.

III.   Manner of how sounds are produced

Nasals- There are three sounds that make up nasal sounds {m, n, and g}. All nasal sounds are voiced and are produced as the airstream is directed through the nasal passage. For an example practice saying mat, nature, and general.

Glides- There are three sounds which are glides {j,w,r}. Glides move towards the vowel sound that follows. The Chinese often have difficulty pronouncing the "r" correctly at the middle and end of a word. For an example practice saying jam, wrist, rose, mirror, and washer.

Stops/Plosives- These sounds {p,b}, {t,d}, {k,g} stop the airstream completely and then release it.

Fricatives- These sounds {s,z}, {θ, ð},{v,f,},{ʃ, dʒ} are produced by forcing the airstream through a narrow passage. Mandarin speakers often find that sounds in this category are difficult to produce. Many speakers frequently leave the "s" endings of words off. Let's discuss production of these important sounds in detail.

{s, z} to produce these sounds, you must raise the middle, and sides of your tongue and form a central channel. You must force the air between the tip of the tongue. The "s" sound is unvoiced, and there is no vibration in the vocal folds, and the "z" sound there is voiced and there is a vibration in the vocal folds. For an example practice saying south and zeal.

{θ, ð}="th" to produce these sounds you must place your tongue tip on the lower edge of your top teeth to block air. You then will force air over the surface of the tongue while pulling tongue back. The "θ" sound is unvoiced and the "ð" sound is voiced. For an example practice saying theory and there.

{v,f} and {s,z} to produce these sounds, you are to rest your lower edges of your top teeth on your bottom lip as you release a stream of air. The air released is a continuous sound, such as the words "very" and "ferry". For an example practice saying ratting and loose.

Affricates- These sounds "tʃ", such as "cheese" and /dʒ/, such as "judge", are a combination of a stop and a vibrating fricative sound. For example, /tʃ/ is a voiceless palatal sound. It is characterized by tensing the lips and pushing them forward. You should bring the teeth together, blocking the air by putting the tip and sides of the tongue to the roof of your mouth. Open your mouth and release the air, saying the words "cherry" and "jump".

Liquids- These sounds {r, l} have some features of vowels and consonants. The "r" sound, has the lips rounded and the tip is curled upward, pointing towards the roof of the mouth. The vocal folds are vibrating. The "l" sound, places the tongue at the ridge behind the center top teeth. You are to push the air up from the throat through the nose, vibrating the vocal cords.

BLENDS AND CLUSTERS

The Consonant clusters and blends, as well as omission of final sounds are challenging areas for Mandarin speakers. Consonant blends and clusters can occur at the beginning, middle, and endings of words.

When pronouncing consonant blends, the letters are always pronounced, one after the other without being separated. The two most common cluster difficulties among Chinese speakers are the {l- clusters} and {r-clusters}. There are many additional cluster patterns and formations; however we will focus on the 10 most common.

R- clusters

Br	cr	fr	str	thr
Brain	cream	frog	string	throat
Break	cram	frown	straw	throb
Bright	crystal	friend	street	three
Brisk	crazy	front	strive	thick

L –clusters

Bl	cl	fl	gl	sl
Bliss	class	float	gloomy	slab
Blond	cloth	fluid	glass	sleep
Bloom	clear	flap	glove	slice
Black	clinic	flame	glue	slip

Practicing repeating each consonant cluster phrase several times. You will want to stop the recording to listen to how the words are pronounced. Try practicing these phrases varying your rate of speed. You can record yourself for additional practice.

CONSONANT CLUSTER PHRASES

1. Break a lease
2. Crystal clear
3. Front and center
4. Strawberries and cream
5. Thick and thin
6. Black and white
7. Class clown
8. Slip and slide
9. Breakfast cereal
10. Break the rules
11. Bride and groom
12. Crime and punishment
13. Thunder and Lightening
14. Stars and stripes

HOW VOWELS ARE PRODUCED   TRACK 6

The pronunciations of American vowels are very challenging for Mandarin speakers. It is interesting to notice how your tongue, lips, and facial muscles change when you pronounce vowels. To experience how changing the lips and tongue muscles have an effect on the words, view your vowel production chart and practice the sounds and words. When you start at the top and work your way down the list, you will notice the sounds are initially high front and unrounded. Practice saying these words and notice how your lips and tongue change position:

{Beat, bit, bait, bet, bat, bot, but, Baul, bowl, bull, bool}

Vowels are always produced with voicing with air flow through the mouth continuously unless it is stopped by a consonant. To experience this say the word, "flee", and then pronounce "fleet". It is important to note that correct vowel production is based on the positions of the tongue, lips, and the tension of the facial muscles.

- Tongue position is based on the location and height.
- Lip position is either rounded or unrounded
- Facial muscles are tense or relaxed.

It is best to categorize how the vowels are produced: Diphthongs, Front, Back, and Central vowels. Diphthongs involve a combination of two blended sounds that don't stand alone.

Knowing how individual vowel sounds are produced will help with English pronunciation. You will want to refer to the vowel formation chart on the next page which helps you determine where the vowels are produced in the mouth.

VOWEL FORMATION CHART

FRONT VOWELS

Vowel Sounds	Target Words	Position of Lips	Position of Tongue	Facial Muscles
i	Me	Unrounded	High	Tense
ɪ	Hit	Unrounded	High	Relaxed
e	Bait	Unrounded	High	Tensed
ɛ	Let	Unrounded	High	Relaxed
ae	Sat	Unrounded	High	Relaxed

CENTRAL VOWELS

	Target Words	Position of Lips	Position of Tongue	Facial Muscles
ʌ	Bun	Unrounded	Mid	Relaxed
ə	Alike	Unrounded	Mid	Relaxed
ɝ	Work	Rounded	Mid	Tense
ɚ	Labor	Rounded	mid	Tense

BACK VOWELS

	Target Words	Position of Lips	Position of Tongue	Facial Muscles
U	Cool	Rounded	High	Tense
ʊ	Look	Rounded	High	Relaxed
o	Soap	Rounded	High	Tense
ɑ	Box	Unrounded	Low	Relaxed
ɔ	Saw	Unrounded	Low	Relaxed

ENGLISH SOUNDS NOT PRESENT IN THE MANDARIN LANGUAGE

There are several English sounds that do not naturally occur in the Mandarin language. Knowing which English sounds that are not in your native language allows you to focus on them systematically through speech discrimination practice. Chinese speakers frequently have difficulty with vowel English contrasts, so it will be important to listen to the recording several times, and stopping to practice throughout the day.

"g"   fog   (final position)

"v"   vote   (initial position)

"z"   zeal   (initial position)

"ʃ" shy   sh= ʃ

"ʒ" beige   ʒ= ge

"tʃ" chew   tʃ=ch

"dʒ" jaw   dz-j

"θ" think   θ=th (unvoiced)

"ð" this   ð=th (voiced)

"h" hard

No final {t, l, or b}

Challenging Consonants

"L" (initial position)

"w" (initial position)

"s" (initial position)

"v" (initial position)

"z" (final position)

"s" (initial position)

"r" (initial, medial, and final positions)

<u>Challenging Vowels</u>

"u" vs. "ʊ" {pool/pull}

"i" vs "ɪ" {reach/rich}

"ʌ" vs "ae" {cup/cap}

"a" vs "ae" {cop/cap}

"e" vs "ɛ" {wait/wet}

Week 2

SHARPENING YOUR LISTENING SKILLS — TRACK 7

After working with many students, I have discovered that it is difficult for my students to produce certain English sounds because it is hard to perceive them. Learning how to discriminate among sounds that are not pronounced in your native language will take some practice. Listen and practice this session frequently.

<u>Practicing minimum Pairs and Speech Discrimination</u>

1. When you are practicing the minimum pair combination, it is best to initially listen to the recording and following along in the workbook. Repeat this step several times to get familiar with the words.
2. Your next step is to listen to the recording without looking at the words. Listen to the words, stop the recording and practice. Your main objective is to focus on the words and how they are pronounced, carefully imitating the voice on the recording.
3. If you are experiencing difficulty with this step, review how the sounds are produced in the mouth and begin again with these speech discrimination tasks.

<u>Single word exercises</u>

1. Take a look at the words in the workbook and listen to how they are pronounced on the recording. It's important to train your ear on how the words sound and imitate the words several times a day.

2. It can be very helpful to look at the words and think of a word that is associated with it. For example, if the target word is berry, think of a word that is associated with berry, such as "strawberry, or blueberry". Practice saying the target word, and add the associated word. You can make a recording of yourself while doing this fun exercise for additional practice.

Sentences & Paragraphs

1. Listen to the sentences on the recording. Listen to the phrasing, rate of speech, and intonation of how each sentence sounds. You will want to listen to each sentence, stop the recording and repeat each sentence several times.
2. Listen to how the words are flowing together and word association patterns. Take the time and practice on your fluency while pronouncing the target words with accuracy.
3. For additional practice, you will want to record yourself while doing this activity.

VOWEL SPEECH DISCRIMINATION

PRACTICING MINIMUM PAIRS (SPEECH DISCRIMINATION) — **TRACK 8**

"i" Vowel

i/ ɪ
- meet - mitt
- beef - bit
- seek - sick
- greed - grid

Practice Words

1. Streak
2. Greeting
3. Speak
4. Keep
5. Leaky
6. Teach
7. Redeem
8. Piece

Practice Sentences

1. Why don't you eat a piece of beef and drink some tea.
2. Eve will make a speech before she starts to teach.
3. She will make a greeting to the Greek team.
4. Be careful when you cross the clean street.

"æ" Vowel

a/ æ   cop   -   cap
         hot   -   hat
         lock   -   lack
         smock   -   smack

Practice words

1. Pack
2. Bracket
3. Chance
4. Sack
5. Rack
6. Chance
7. Black
8. Jack

Practice Sentences

1. Jack wants the cash from the lamp sale in the gallery.
2. The jazz band played wearing black hats while sitting in the van.
3. I have to pass on attending the art class before I graduate.
4. Patty put on her drab jacket before her date with Dan.

"e" Vowel

e/ ɛ	bait	-	bet
	gate	-	get
	lace	-	let
	rake	-	wreck

Practice Words

1. Played
2. Bake
3. Bacon
4. Safe
5. Table
6. Shade
7. Lake
8. Obey

Practice Sentences

1. David loved to bake cakes and have parties at the lake.
2. Your eight children love to play and skate all day.
3. The baby was delivered late while they found a safe place to stay.
4. The potato was prepared with bacon and given to the matron.

"ʊ" Vowel

u/ ʊ   pool   -   pull
          cool   -   could
          fool   -   full
          smooth   -   should

Practice words

1. Look
2. Brook
3. Shook
4. Crook
5. Good
6. Would
7. Bull
8. Push

Practice Sentences

1. I wish you would not stand on my bad foot.
2. Butch pushed the bushel of books behind the cushion.
3. Tara was up to no good when she put the sugar on the horse's hoof.
4. We sat by the brook while Butch cooked us a full meal.

Week 2

CONSONANT SPEECH DISCRIMINATION

MINIMUM PAIRS (SPEECH DISCRIMINATION) — TRACK 9

Initial consonant: "p"

Remember to put your lips together to stop the air, part the lips, then release the air in a quick burst.

p/b	pie	-	bye
	pony	-	bony
	peach	-	beach
	pin	-	bin

Practice Words

1. Pig
2. Paid
3. Pea
4. People
5. Pocket
6. Police
7. Paris
8. Pale

Practice Sentences

1. You can't bring any pets in that part of the building.
2. I bet you put a lot of money in the big purse.
3. Please take the back path to Paul's house.
4. Peter loves to read poems and paint at his beach house.

Final consonant: "t"

Remember to partially part your lips (pretend you are smiling), then place your tongue behind your front teeth, allowing the air to be released quickly. This sound involves no vocal fold vibration.

t / d	seat	-	seed
	shot	-	shod
	riot	-	rode
	blot	-	blood

Practice Words

1. Fleet
2. Suit
3. Cheat
4. Quart
5. Treat
6. Write
7. Riot
8. Vote

Practice Sentences

1. Matt played the flute at the state conference center.
2. Why don't you treat your wife to a new suit coat?
3. Pat wrote about the riots and the gun shot.
4. That man is a liar and a cheat.

Initial consonant: "ð" (voiced th)

Remember to put tongue tip in the middle of your top teeth to block air and then you force air around the tongue as you pull the tongue back quickly. This causes the vocal folds to vibrate

d/ ð   den   -   then
       day   -   they
       dare -   their
       die   -   thy

Practice Words

1. These   5. Thou
2. They   6. There
3. The   7. Theory
4. This   8. That

Practice Sentences

1. You wouldn't dare put that door over there.
2. This den is painted a deeper color than the kitchen.
3. They say that Theodore tested a sound theory.
4. The chair and this couch match.

Initial consonants: "z"

Remember you are to raise your middle and sides of the tongue, to form a channel. You are to force air through the channel, causing the vocal folds to vibrate as air passes through the channel.

s/z	sink	-	zinc
	seal	-	zeal
	sip	-	zip
	sewn	-	zone

Practice Words

1. Zodiac
2. Zebra
3. Zone
4. Zipcode
5. Zipper
6. Zoo
7. Zion
8. Zeal

Practice Sentences

1. Why don't you get ready to go to the zoo to photograph zebras.
2. His clothes always have two zippers that need to be zipped.
3. The peas and rice was served by Zelma.
4. Why don't you please tell me your zodiac sign?

Initial consonants: "θ" (unvoiced 'th')

Remember you are to put your tongue on your lower top teeth, and block the air. Your vocal folds do not vibrate as you are to force air over tongue surface.

s/ θ	saw	-	thaw
	some	-	thumb
	sink	-	think
	seem	-	theme

Practice words

1. Thirsty
2. Thesis
3. Think
4. Thump
5. Thing
6. Thought
7. Thermal
8. Thunder

Practice Sentences

1. The rain and thunder lasted until 10:30.
2. Why don't you do something about your math thesis?
3. Let's go to the theatre on the third Thursday of the month.
4. I'll stay with you through thick and thin.

Final consonants: "v"

Remember, place your top teeth on lower lip to block the air, and push air out of the opening causing the air to travel up and the vocal folds to vibrate

v/f   believe - belief

leave - leaf

dove - loaf

drive - five

Practice words

1. Sleeve
2. Dove
3. Drive
4. Prove
5. Glove
6. Love
7. Wave
8. Stove

Practice Sentences

1. Why don't you and Steve leave the stove in the corner?
2. I love to drive to the Star cave which is five miles from my house.
3. What can you do to prove you love me?
4. I purchased twelve stoves to give away at the Waver charity event.

Week  3

WORD ASSOCIATIONS & CONTRACTIONS — TRACK 10

Phrasing & Linking Longer Messages

Many times you are linking a list of items and linking two or more short messages into one. What's the best way to do this? When linking phrases, each phrase will end on a rising pitch up to the last phrase, which ends using a falling inflection. These rules will also apply to questions.

Listen to the examples and practice these sentences exactly as the speaker pronounces them.

1. I'd like to drive to Vermont, but I'm not sure if I can.
2. Tom cut three apples, two bananas, and four oranges for the sangria.
3. Did the children play on the new swing, jump on the pogo stick, or swim in the pool?

To review from last week, it's important to note that each thought contains one primary stress point. You cannot apply the stress rules of your native language onto English speech unless it is the same, otherwise the results are disastrous.

The Use of Contractions

Contractions are a shortening of a word or phrase by the omission of one or more letters. The use of contractions will result in speech that is more fluid and natural. American's use contractions automatically and is used frequently in casual conversation. There are many contractions; here are a few to start using in your daily conversations.

Here are some common Contractions

We are	We're
can not	Can't
Should not	Shouldn't
She has	She's
We have	We've
I have	I've
Do not	Don't
You are	Your're
I am	I'm
It is	It's
What is	What's
I had	I'd
I will	I'll
He will	He'll
Had not	Hadn't
Could not	Couldn't
Have not	Haven't
Would not	Wouldn't
Has not	Hasn't
Will not	Won't
Is not	Isn't
Might not	Mightn't
Need not	Needn't
Are not	Aren't
Here is	Here's

Week 4

THE IMPORTANCE OF INTONATION — TRACK 11

There are so many aspects of communication in all languages. There are many clues when you observe body language and facial expressions. For example, you can tell if someone is happy or sad often by looking at their facial expressions and body language. English pronunciation involves grammar rules and gives clarity to individual speech sounds and words. The flow and tempo of speech is known as speech rhythm. Speech rhythm, which includes intonation, involves stress, pitch, rate of speech, and duration.

When correct intonation patterns are used with English pronunciation, the listener understands the message faster and can respond much more quickly. If the correct pattern is not used, the listener needs a lot more time to figure out the message. Communication can become frustrating for both the speaker and listener.

Many Chinese speakers, often don't recognize how critical the rhythm and flow of the English language is to meaning. When an American initially hears the Mandarin accent, many times there is the lack of the rhythm and flow of speech. Without intonation, the speech sounds flat and mechanical.

Native Chinese speakers often speak word by word and stress each word equally, which can make the speech sound unnatural. To learn the American English accent is not only about pronunciation, it's about using correct intonation patterns. Let's discuss stress and pitch which are critical components of intonation and why they are so important.

Stress:

Stress involves placing the emphasis on a word to make it stand out from everything else spoken in the message. This is done by using a higher pitch or using a louder voice. There are three stress levels in American English: the first or initial level, the 2nd level, and the final level or soft. The first level is the strongest; the second level is less strong than the 1st. The final level (or soft) receives the least amount of stress. Listen to the word, "**poi**son". In the following exercises, the initial level of stress will be in a larger font and the secondary level of stress in a word will be noted in *italics*.

<u>Stress Patterns in Words</u>

There are three ways a speaker stresses a word:

1. The first way is to use a louder voice
2. The second way is to use a higher pitch
3. The third way is to use the voice to stretch out the word.

Here are some guidelines that will help you understand and apply the patterns and use them with English pronunciation.

a. The prefix or suffixes of words are not stressed. Noun, verbs, and adjectives of at least two syllables are stressed on first syllable. For example: **gov**ernor, **geo**metry

b. Stress is placed on the part of the word that is the most critical to the overall meaning of the word. Stress can be anywhere in the word, including the middle such as un**natu**ral

c. The initial word in a compound word is typically stressed. For example: **Foot**ball **Snow**ball **Cup**cake **Grey**hound

d. For suffixes starting with the letter i, stress is typically placed on the syllable before the suffix. For example listen to the recording and repeat the following words: *as***so***ciate*, **fash**ion, and **ben**eficiary

Suffixes:

- iate
- iable
- io
- ion
- ic
- ive
- iant
- ify
- ial
- iar
- ish
- ily
- iary

Let's practice the Stress Patterns in Words

Remember the primary stress level will be illustrated with a larger font and the secondary level of stress will be in italics. Let's start our practice session. Listen carefully for the stress patterns in the following words.

Head*light*

L**ar**gest

re**bel**ion

Actress

Opinion

pres**ump**tion

pres**tige**

re**bel**

Topcoat

Hairbrush

re**Peat**

di**rec**tion

s**car**let

se**cre**tion

suc**ces**sive

STRESS PATTERNS IN SENTENCES

The stress patterns in sentences are the result of the position of the stress and unstressed syllables. When you practice with using stress patterns in phrases and sentences, you will need to know that words may be stressed for emphasis, such as **No**, you can't go to the party. Here are a couple of rules to follow:

1. Words that are prepositions, articles, pronouns are not stressed. Words that have content and meaning such as nouns, adjectives, adverbs, and verbs are stressed.

2. If you are asking a question, and starting the sentence with How, why, when, what, where, and who, these words are stressed in questions. You are also to using a rising tone at the end of the question.

Pitch:

Mandarin Chinese is a tonal language. There are four tones in Mandarin Chinese. Americans speak words using various tones from high to low. In American English, there are four levels of pitch in speech. Level 1 (Primary) usually starts the sentence and can reflect emotional lows. Level 4 (very high pitch), is often used to express high emotions such as surprise. When you listen to native speakers, you will notice the pitch is up all the time especially when new information is introduced in a sentence.

If someone asks a question you will notice, the voice is raised at the end of the sentence. In other words, pitch tells the listener the intention of the speaker and where the speaker is in the sentence. The tone shifts in English are very similar to those in Chinese. The Americans use the shifts to indicate stress and a change in tone for the Chinese indicates a different word. It's important to note that Chinese grammar is very similar to English.

Intonation Patterns

After students have been working with me for a few weeks, I often have them prepare a five to ten minute speech about a favorite holiday, how to prepare their favorite meal, or to reflect on a pleasant experience. They are not to memorize the speech, but to deliver the speech to me using their best grammar. This session is recorded and played back to review. If the student sounds mechanical or is speaking word by word, we start working on how to form word connections.

Here's a passage given to me from one of my students.

Spring Festival Day

"If anyone asks me what my favorite festival in my country is, no doubt, it is Spring Festival Day. The reasons are many, and apparently because it is the symbol of Chinese culture. You can experience the authentic traditional Chinese culture and happy atmosphere on this day. What's more, it is also the day of reunion in China.

People get together with their family no matter where they are. Children are probably the happiest creatures in the world because they get gifts from their parents and relatives. In order to celebrate this special moment of the year, people will leave their house and visit their relatives in exchange for the best regards on the following days." Meng Ge

---

Remember, using intonation can reveal how you feel. You may read the former passage and have experienced a bad day or feeling sad at the moment. Your stress and pitch level may be much lower that day than usual, so there is no right or wrong way. Practice reading the passage imitating the intonation patterns of the speaker. The importance of the exercise is to practice using variable stress and pitch levels of words to change meaning.

Let's practice the difference in intonation with a question versus a statement. When Native Americans ask questions, they will have a rising intonation pattern at the end. A statement will have the same intonation pattern, but the pitch will not be as high at the end. Please listen to the following.

1. Here is my new scarf. – Statement
2. Where is my new **scarf?** - Question

Intonation can also rise in an emotional situation. Please listen, "Where is my bike? Why is it gone? Practice these 4 sentences and pay attention to the pitch changes which will vary the meaning.

1. I'm tired of the **rain.**
2. It **looks** like it may rain today.
3. John **likes** pizza, but he **hates** hotdogs.
4. He **can't give** me a failing grade.

Here's one of my favorite exercises to give students. I will have 5 sentences and each student is to translate the sentences into their native language and practice saying the sentences stressing a different word every time they say it. Here are 5 sentences to translate in your native language. Listen as each sentence is read twice, each time stressing a different word.

1. The table looks wet.
2. Listen to that response.
3. Please pass the salt.
4. Shall I get you a cup of coffee?
5. Is it five o'clock yet?

American intonation consists of multiple pitch levels, very high and very low. It is always best to focus on how words sound and used together, not on the spelling. Work very hard to listen to words and to pay attention to the context in which the words are used.

Week 5

PRACTICE STORIES — TRACK 12

Practice stories

These funny stories are created for additional practice. These stories are phonetically loaded with the target phoneme. The characters and the stories are fictitious. Any reference to real names and locations are coincidental and unintentional. As mentioned previously, Chinese speakers usually have difficulty pronouncing "R" in the initial, medial, and final positions.

If you have difficulties with the consonants (R,L) refer to the American Consonant sounds chart. These stories can help you with word associations and fluency. You are to initially read sentences and then read the sentences in a paragraph working on linking the words together to increase fluency. You may want to stop the audio several times to work on different goals such as rate of speech, intonation, and pronunciation.

Week 5

| #1 PRACTICE STORY | TRACK 13 |

INITIAL "R"

"R" REGGIE ROBERTS

Pronunciation Rules: This is a voiced sound. The tongue tip may or may not be elevated. The lips may or may not be rounded. You will need to raise the middle of the tongue to the roof of the mouth to stop the air. Direct the airstream over the tongue and out the mouth, vibrating the vocal folds. You should be able to sustain this sound for a long time if you have done this correctly.

1. Reggie Roberts lived in Reno, Nevada and loved to raise his dear rabbits in a rose colored room in his home.
2. Everyday Reggie would run his rabbits on a mirrored obstacle course he built right outside his residence.
3. He would feed them a diet of raw carrots, raisins, and plenty of raspberries that were prepared in a sherry sauce.
4. Reggie would give the rabbits plenty of rest and water after the required daily regimen.
5. One day, Reggie decided to revise the routine and they all retired and moved to the Renaissance Resort without any regret.
6. In October, the mayor was inspired by Reggie and gave him a party.
7. Reggie was presented with an award.
8. After receiving the award, Reggie was able to star in an upcoming movie role, which was titled,"The Warrior and the Rabbit".

Reggie Roberts lived in Reno, Nevada and loved to raise his dear rabbits in a rose colored room in his home. Everyday Reggie would run his rabbits on a mirrored obstacle course he built right outside his residence. He would feed them a diet of raw carrots, raisins, and plenty of raspberries that were prepared in a sherry sauce. Reggie would give the rabbits plenty of rest and water after the required daily regimen. One day, Reggie decided to revise the routine and they all retired and moved to the Renaissance Resort without any regret. In October, the mayor was inspired by Reggie and gave him a party. Reggie was presented with an award. After receiving the award, Reggie was able to star in an upcoming movie role, which was titled, "The warrior and the rabbit".

#2 PRACTICE STORY — TRACK 14

Final "L"

"L"   Kelly and Kyla

Pronunciation Rules: The final /l/ sound is challenging for Mandarin speakers. You will need to keep the tongue tip raised. The tongue has to be at the ridge behind center top teeth, then push air from throat and out through nose releasing it.

1. Kelly and Kyla were two cousins who owned a doll store a mile from our school.
2. Every day the two girls would drive a mile through the tunnel to visit our school.
3. The girl's daily goal was to sell several dolls at our school.
4. Each doll was dressed in a unique style and wore a smile.
5. Eventually, the girls sold their business in the fall to purchase a kennel in Mobile, Alabama.
6. Kelly applied to Yale University and won a full scholarship.
7. Kyla decided to remain in Mobile, Alabama after the fall to run the business.
8. Both girls decided it was a little late in life to be truly loyal to the business, and they took their lifelong earnings to Lake Powell to live.

Kelly and Kyla were two cousins who owned a doll store a mile from our school. Every day the two girls would drive a mile through the tunnel to visit our school. The girl's daily goal was to sell several dolls at our school. Each doll was dressed in a unique style and wore a smile. Eventually, the girls sold their business in the fall to purchase a kennel in Mobile, Alabama. Kelly applied to Yale University and won a full scholarship. Kyla decided to remain in Mobile, Alabama after the fall to run the business. Both girls decided it was a little late in life to be truly loyal to the business, and they took their lifelong earnings to Lake Powell to live.

Week 6

AMERICAN IDIOMATIC EXPRESSIONS & PHRASES — TRACK 15

Like it or not, the American workplace and most social scenes are full of colorful idioms and expressions. People don't begin a project; they get a project off the ground. Many professionals who work in teams don't just talk about ideas or brainstorm; they like to run some ideas by us!

Many foreign born individuals who speak English as a second language, including the Chinese don't recognize how important idioms are. You will need to get comfortable using idioms. How is this best accomplished? There is no one way to do it. It takes some time and practice. When they come up in conversation and you don't understand, the best way is to write them down. You can ask an American who speaks well to explain the meaning. You will also be able to practice at the end of this session.

Check out newspapers, for example the Wall Street Journal, and business sections of the daily newspapers are full of these idioms. Eventually, when they come up in conversation, you'll be soon prepared to respond confidently, instead of becoming silent while thinking to yourself, "What are they talking about now?"

How often have you heard these common expressions, "they pulled the plug," "let's keep in touch", or "it slipped my mind?" The use of idioms will add color and excitement to your language, help you develop a deeper meaning of the English language, and make you sound more like a native speaker.

Practice using these commonly used idioms for fluency. Try using one of these idioms throughout the day for the next 7 weeks. For extra practice, try listening to the audio and record yourself saying the selected idiom and use the idiom in a new sentence.

IDIOM used in a sentence	Meaning
Best shot I studied every day to pass the bar exam, and gave it my best shot.	I tried as hard as I could
Think outside the box Did you think outside of the box on your project?	To think creatively in a new way
Sleep on it Thanks for the proposal, let me sleep on it.	To think about a decision overnight; to decide on something important
Out of my system I'm glad I tried the summer internship program and got that out of my system.	To experience something to one's satisfaction or contentment
Stepping Stone Jerry views her position as the head computer programmer as a stepping stone to much larger projects.	An activity that comes first and paves the road for what will come next.
Get his foot in the door Although the Animal shelter was not hiring, Larry decided to volunteer, so he could get his foot in the door.	To work for an organization, often this can lead to increased opportunities
Burned out After Mary completed her Master's degree, she felt burned out.	To be very tired, to lose effectiveness due to the longevity or intensity of a situation
Up to speed Now that I'm back from vacation, I need to get up to speed on the new project	Learn how to do a new task
Hands are tied I would like to get you the promotion but, my hands are tied.	I'm stuck, I can't do anything
Show of hands Let me see a show of hands on how many people voted in Tuesday's election	To get an actual count (How many)

Week 6

IDIOM used in a sentence	Meaning
Passed with flying colors Mildred completed all four classes and passed with flying colors	She had no difficulty. To do exceptionally well.
Kill time Mary arrived 1 hour early to her interview, so she went to the pottery store to kill time.	To keep herself busy until her appointment/appointed time.
What's up? What's up? It's great to see you again	What's new & what's happening
People person Berry is such a friendly people person, we should hire him immediately.	Someone who loves people
Under the weather Mary had to call in sick because she was under the weather.	Under the weather=Not feeling too well
No hard feelings Tom has no hard feelings from the breakup with his girlfriend.	No anger and no bitterness
Wearing many hats Julia has a new company and she's wearing may hats	To perform many roles and duties
Stomach is killing me & Sick as a dog My stomach is killing me and I'm sick as a dog because I ate my own cooking.	It can be "stomach, arm, leg, or any body part) Not feeling well
Ripped off Julia was ripped off over $2000 when she placed her order at the fabric store.	To steal, and to rob
Throw in the towel After working 12 years on the project, Jeff finally decided to throw in the towel	To call it quits. To admit defeat

Week  7

WEEK 7   **TRACK 16**

Tips on building an Advanced Level Vocabulary

It is possible to communicate effectively without using a lot of very big words. In fact, one never completes vocabulary acquisition; it is a lifelong process for everyone. So, what is the big deal anyway about building an advanced level vocabulary? Any time we start using new words and phrases we start expanding our mind into new areas. Every day we use new words, we become more fluid as we continue to explore the world around us.

Memorization & Word Associations

1. One of the best methods to build a vocabulary for a second language successfully is to use word memorization techniques. If one word is visually or phonetically associated with another word, it is a lot easier to remember. Visualize the word in its printed form. Say the word aloud, and spell it aloud. Say a sentence aloud that uses the new word. Make up an image in your mind that will help you remember the word.

2. Of course, many times there is not another word that can easily be associated with the newly learned vocabulary word. Word association techniques can be very limited at times, and it may take one a long time to learn and apply new vocabulary words.

3. Practice makes perfect and the more you work at this, the easier it becomes. Continue to practice associating new words with words in your primary language.

Read more Books

1. There are many other methods to expanding your vocabulary, however if you start reading books and articles that are slightly more advanced that what you are presently used to, you will start to expand. It really doesn't matter if it is fiction or nonfiction.

2. You will increase your understanding of words by reading more books. Get in the habit of reading new material every day. Look for ways to challenge yourself and stay involved.

Carry your dictionary & utilize online resources

1. As you begin to read more, you will come across words that you do not know. It's understandable. Be sure to keep your pocket dictionary handy. If you don't carry a dictionary, please check out some online dictionaries. One of my favorite online dictionary is the Merriam-Webster which will also help you pronounce words.

2. There are several online dictionaries, and many are for specialties, such as scientists or educators, but there are many more for everyone else. The Merriam-Webster online dictionary has a great feature that you can sign up for "word of the day". It's a nice feature to receive a new word every day. It's even more important to actually try to use the word of the day as often as possible. There will be some words that don't apply to you, but during the week, there will be at least one or two that you can start to use in everyday conversations.

3. Finally, when you encounter a new word, write out a definition of it in your own words, and write one or more sentences using the new word in context. Don't wait and try to do this later, you'll naturally forget about it. So, get in the habit of looking up words that you are not familiar with and find out their meaning. You will also try to associate that new word with one in your native language for faster recall.

Parting Words

I hope you enjoyed *7 weeks to a better American Accent for Native Mandarin Speakers* – volume 1. Take a look at the Resources and the Bonus material. Be sure to visit the blog page http://blog.instituteofaccentmodification.com and check out the articles. Don't forget to sign up for the newsletter. You will be the first to know when new programs and materials become available. I welcome your feedback, which will make this a better series.

RESOURCES

1. For more information on ordering additional books or materials, and to inquire about the author guest speaking for your organization, visit www.sovereignlanguagepress.com or call (888) 827-4479

2. For more information on the comprehensive speech analysis, customized programs and workshops, visit www.instituteofaccentmodification.com

3. Read aloud daily. Read outside your area of knowledge and tape record yourself

4. Look for every opportunity to practice your spoken American English several times a day for 10-15 minutes. My best students practice for an hour each day in small increments.

5. Find others who speak English as a second language such as Meet up groups and language specific groups in local colleges and universities.

6. Have a goal each time you practice. For example, the first practice session of the day, you may only focus on the pronunciation, paying close attention to the rules of how to pronounce the target sound correctly. The next practice session you can have a goal of using the target sound in a phase and a sentence. The next practice session you can practice fluency by repeating the sentences.

7. Visit and join a local Toastmasters meeting. Toastmasters.org is an international organization for people from all walks of life who want to improve their communication/presentation skills.

8. Check out www.merriam-webster.com Don't forget to sign up for the word of the day!

BONUS MATERIAL

Improved Presentation Skills & Voice Projection

The Voice that Captivates

Breathing: The First Step toward a Powerful and Captivating Voice

You can speak only as well as you breathe. Control your breath, and you begin to control your speaking voice. Also, better breathing reduces tension in the neck, back, and shoulders that can inhibit your best natural voice. Try the following exercises to work on speaking with increased voice projection.

1. **Get ready.** Stand with your feet not quite shoulder width apart, your weight forward, more on the balls of the feet than the heels. Relax your hands by your sides. Relax your fingertips and start to pay attention to your breathing. As you exhale, release your shoulders, relax your neck, unclench your teeth, and see if you can't manage a yawn and maybe even a smile. Try this exercise for 5-10 minutes daily, especially before you start to speak in front of a group.

2. **Diaphragmatic breathing.** This is breathing from your belly. It fuels your voice and releases tension from your upper body. It's also called belly breathing because as you inhale, your belly expands (and your chest and shoulders don't move). To demonstrate this, you should place one hand over your belly button. Slowly inhale one long breath through your mouth while silently counting "one... two... three... four." Your stomach should greatly expand, pushing your hand forward (your shoulders and chest should not move.)

   Feel your hand move out as you pull the breath deep into your lungs. Now, hold that breath and count silently, "one... two... three... four." Next, exhale the breath through your mouth while counting silently, "one... two... three... four." Do this until you are comfortable and breathing easily. It's important to use your lungs, intercostals muscles, and diaphragm while counting. Now, you are ready to make sound.

3. **Mmm...** You are going to make a gentle "Mmm" sound, using up an entire breath on just that one sound. Take in a full belly breath, and as you exhale say a very gentle and quiet sustained Mmmmmmmmm... until you run out of air. Do it again, being certain to really open your mouth as you softly sustain the Mmmm. Next, practice humming Aaaaahhhh-hhhh more loudly to warm up the articulators.

4. **Reading with emphasis**…..Now that you are all warmed up, look for an advertisement in the newspaper, yellow pages, or brochure. Stand up and read the advertisement aloud and create the emphasis on the service or product being sold. Emphasize the benefits of using the product or service. Practice this exercise in front of a friend or your accent coach, asking them if they are convinced that they should use the service!

5. **Your vocal image & Preparing voice recordings**…..Your voice is an important part of the image you project to your prospective clients, existing clients, work colleagues, and anyone who hears you. It doesn't matter if you are speaking on the phone, face-to-face, or making a public speech. Take the time to analyze your own speaking voice. Are you speaking softly? Does your voice convey confidence? Listen very carefully to the American news reporters on CNN or the local news. Tape record twenty minutes of the evening news and listen to the recording several times. Try to imitate the words, pronunciation, and the rate of speech. If you practice this tip for several weeks, you will improve your English pronunciation and rate of speech.

Anytime you hear your own voice on the tape recorder, you are hearing yourself only through air conduction. This will explain why your voice sounds very different than when you normally speak. When you speak normally, your voice passes through the bones in your neck to your vocal folds, and to your auditory system. The tape recorded voice is what other people hear. Now that you know this important fact, you will need to learn how to adjust your tone and rate of speech for the best result. Seek the help of a speech professional would be very helpful if you are experiencing difficulty.

It's also important to be yourself when communicating. Try to relax your throat when you speak so that a more natural quality will come forth. If you are preparing to speak using a microphone, you will want to practice speaking with the microphone several times before you make your speech. Never get too close to the microphone. You will want to practice making your "p's", and "t's", a little more distance from the microphone. Working on your English pronunciation will take time and dedication. Learn to be patient with the process. Remember, its always better to practice in several short sessions than one long session. This will optimize the transfer of new habits in your everyday speech.

NOTES

NOTES

NOTES

NOTES

NOTES

www.ingramcontent.com/pod-product-compliance
Lightning Source LLC
Chambersburg PA
CBHW081328040426
42453CB00013B/2335